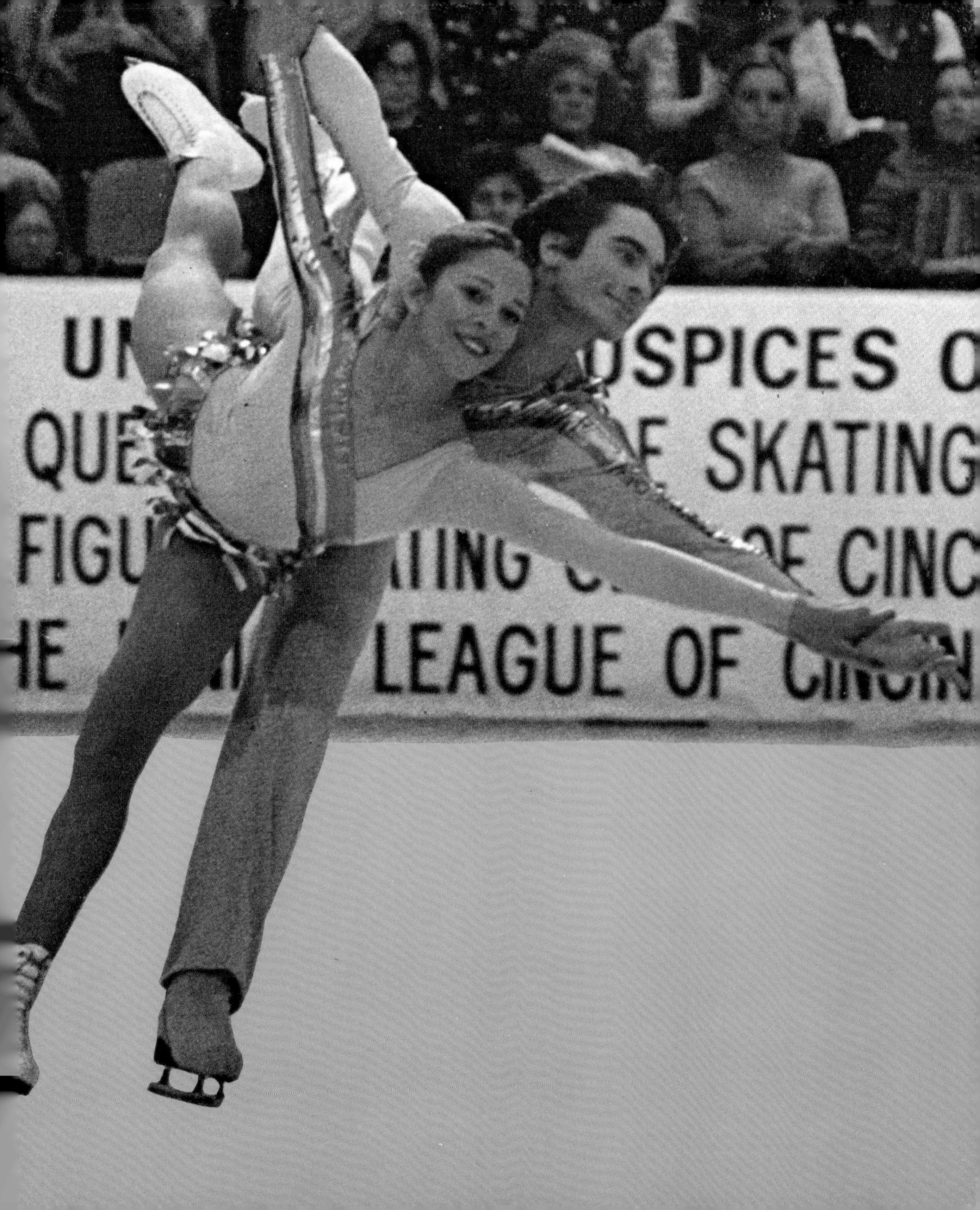
SKATING
LEAGUE OF

Gold Medal Advisory Board

Gregory Smith
Editor in Chief/Skating Magazine
United States Figure Skating Association

Carol Heiss Jenkins
Gold Medalist 1960
Television Commentator/Teacher

Robert Purdy
Executive Director
A.A.U. Bobsledding Association

Thomas E. Hall
Executive Director
Ice Skating Institute
of America

William Markland
Board of Directors/
United States International
Speed Skating Association

Col. F. Donald Miller
Executive Director
United States
Olympic Committee

William D. Traeger
Executive Director
United States Ski Team

Larry Ralston
Permanent Secretary
American Skating Union

Dick Button
Gold Medalist 1948-52
Television Producer/Commentator

Diane Holum
Gold Medalist 1972
Coach/United States Olympic
Speed skating team

Hal Trumble
Executive Director
United States Amateur Hockey Association

George Howie
National Director
United States International Speed Skating Association

OLYMPIC FIGURE SKATING

By the staff of the Ice Skating Institute of America
in cooperation with the United States Olympic Committee

Blairsville Junior High School
Blairsville, Pennsylvania

CHILDRENS PRESS, CHICAGO

Linda Fratianne, United States and World Champion in 1977, won her third United States title in 1979.

Photographs in this book courtesy of the Ice Skating Institute of America, publisher, *XIII Olympic Winter Games, Lake Placid,* © 1979. Created by T.A. Chacharon & Assoc. Ltd.

Cover photograph: Dorothy Hamill, 1976 Olympic gold-medal winner.
Page 1 photograph: Tai Babilonia and Randy Gardner skate their way to their fourth United States national pairs championship in 1979.

LIBRARY OF CONGRESS CATALOGING IN PUBLICATION DATA

Ice Skating Institute of America.
   Olympic figure skating

   SUMMARY: Traces the history of figure skating, the oldest event in the winter Olympic games, and discusses some of the outstanding skaters in this competition and the techniques they have developed over the years.
   1. Skating — Competitions — History — Juvenile literature. 2. Olympic games (winter) — Records — Juvenile literature. 3. Skating — Competitions — Records — Juvenile literature. [1. Ice skating — Competitions — History. 2. Olympic games (winter)] I. United States Olympic Committee. II. Title.
GV850.4.I25   1979   796.9'1   79-16948
ISBN 0-516-02553-8

You stand quietly in the center of a huge arena. There is a hush. The music, *your* music, begins. Every part of you is focused on what you have to do.

You begin your skating routine. First a leap into the air. Remember to land correctly. Moving backward, you leap again and twirl. You move quickly around the rink, building up speed. Remember, this time you have to jump high enough to turn three times in the air. After the leap, you go into a glide, holding your body in a graceful, still pose. You almost dance to the music. You are thinking of your next moves. You concentrate on the moves your body has done many times before. You spin and glide and leap. Every motion must be as perfect as you can make it.

Your music is almost over. The trumpets in it tell you to hurry. The violins remind you to move smoothly. The bass drum gives power to your legs. The flutes put wings on your feet. A final quick spin, a final trumpet blast, and you have finished.

The crowd leaps to its feet and cheers! They tell you with their applause that you have given a performance they will remember for a long time. The judges agree with the crowd—you are an Olympic winner!

Though many skaters set their sights on the Olympics, very few have a chance to experience this special thrill. Each Olympic figure skater must have the strength of a gymnast and the moves of a ballet dancer. Each one must show amazing precision and grace. It is no wonder that figure skating may be the most popular of all the events at the Winter Olympic Games.

In this 16th Century work of Cornelis Dusart, engraved by J. Cole, the early flat skates of Holland are clearly shown, together with the "picked" staff used for propulsion.

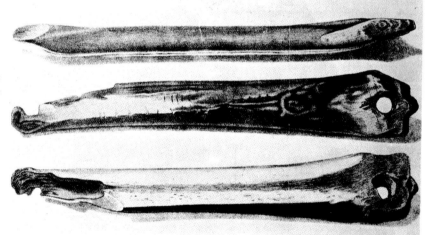

These relics shaped from cow and sheep bones were used to form early skates.

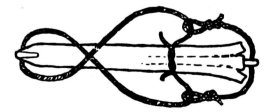

This diagram shows how bones were fastened to boots to form the earliest known skates.

HOW SKATING STARTED

Interest in figure skating has developed only in the last hundred years. Though skating itself is an ancient form of transportation, organized contests and shows have changed it to an exciting, enjoyable sport.

People have skated for hundreds of years. Skating was used as a way to travel in frozen lands, especially those of northern Europe and North America.

The first skates were made of polished animal bones and were strapped to a shoe. In the 1300s the Dutch improved skates by making them with wood. By the 1800s the first iron skates had appeared. Later came steel skates that were clamped, instead of strapped, to a shoe. In the late 1800s, skates as we know them today were developed. These skates have the blade screwed onto the boot, making one unit.

When skates were improved, people began to discover that skating could be fun. Skating with other people, performing difficult moves on ice, and dancing on ice grew more and more popular. Members of royalty amused themselves by skating in the winter. Skating became even more widespread with the invention of refrigerated ice rinks. Then people could skate all year round.

Skating clubs were formed in many countries. The first group formed to regulate skating as an organized sport was started in 1879 in Great Britain. Soon all the countries where skating was popular had such groups. In 1892 these organizations joined together to form the International Skating Union (ISU). The ISU set up rules for skating competitions. This organization still governs international competitions in figure skating, speed skating, and ice dancing. The countries

The famous "Sonja Stop."

Revolutionary jumps and leaps.

Sonja demonstrating her style in 1934.

Sonja was described
by her first movie:
One in a Million.

Skiing and dancing were the activities that led Sonja Heine to skating. Here, at the age of eleven, she entered world competition.

governed by the ISU began to hold national skating championships. Soon there were international championships, too.

Although the modern Olympics began in 1896, figure skating was not made part of the program until 1908. It was a Summer Olympic event until the first Winter Olympic Games were held in 1924.

When figure skating first became a competitive sport, it was very different from the way we now see it. The performance of figures was more important than free skating. Until 1976 compulsory (required) figures counted 60 percent of a skater's final score.

Gradually, free skating became more important. It now counts as 50 percent of a skater's score. In the early years men's free skating was more ''free'' than women's. Men could do athletic leaps, spins, and jumps, while women were supposed to show gliding, feminine grace. It was not until the 1920s that Sonja Heine paved the way for more freedom in women's figure skating. This figure-skating champion from Norway, using spins and jumps that formerly were done only by men, changed forever the way women were expected to skate.

Skate boots must be the correct size. Larger skates cannot be "made" to fit properly by the use of heavy socks.

So that the skate boot with blade attached can act as an extension of the skater's body, the boot must be laced properly. The laces should be loose around the toes, tight over the ankle and instep, and snug, but not tight, near the top of the skate.

The lace should be knotted and the ends tucked inside the boot for safety.

This front view of a figure skate shows the upward curve of the blade that allows only the two outer edges to touch the ice.

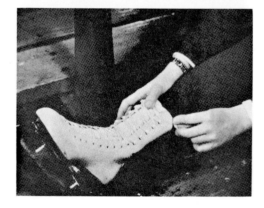

This side view of a figure skate shows the toe picks at the front of the blade.

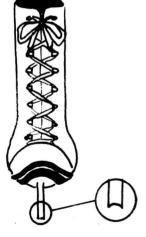

SKATES AND SKATING TECHNIQUES

It is easier to understand figure skating if you understand what a figure skate is.

Figure skates are boots with a single straight piece of steel about ⅛″ thick screwed to the soles. The boot is tall enough to cover the ankles and is usually made of leather. It is reinforced around the heel and the instep of the foot. The skate should be laced fairly loosely around the toes and the top of the boot. It should be laced very tightly over the ankle and the instep. A properly laced skate supports the ankle, and the boot feels like part of the foot.

The blade of the skate is placed slightly closer to the inside of the boot than to the center. The front of the blade has toe picks—a few sharp teeth that can cut into the ice. The blade itself is "hollow-ground." This means that the middle of the blade curves upward. When the blade is flat on the ice, only the two outer edges of the blade touch the surface of the ice.

In performing approved moves, a skater skates on either the inside or the outside edge of the blade. The skater feels much the same way a bicycle rider feels when making a sharp turn and leaning to the right or left. Skaters must also learn to shift their weight forward and backward on each edge. Each skate blade thus has four surfaces—the inside front edge, the inside back edge, the outside front edge, and the outside back edge.

11

*A skater who studies with a special coach
must practice several hours each day.*

TRAINING FOR THE OLYMPICS

Most skaters who compete in the Olympics began to skate for fun. Many children receive a pair of skates as a present. They go to an ice rink to learn how to skate and they find that they like it very much. For most skaters this is enough. They continue to skate just for fun. For a few, however, skating becomes more important. They may have started out by taking classes to learn the basics of the sport and shown exceptional talent. If they are enthusiastic about the sport, and if their parents and instructors agree, they may decide that private lessons would be a good idea. In the United States, private lessons are very expensive. Many families must make sacrifices to give their skaters a chance for further training.

Skaters who start studying with a special coach must practice three hours or more every day. They must also find the time to do their schoolwork and see their friends. Many skaters discover that they are not happy about giving up so much of their time to the sport and don't stay with it. Others continue to learn and practice under the eyes of their coaches.

When a coach and a skater both feel ready, the skater enters skating contests. If the skater does well in local contests, he or she goes on to more and more advanced competitions. Those who are good enough progress to national championships. Skaters under twelve years of age compete in Junior Men's or Women's national championships. Those who are very good are invited to compete in senior-level championship contests. In these contests they compete with skaters who are older than they are. Skaters who do well in these contests go on to international championships.

13

The figure 8 is one of the school figures *often performed as part of the Olympic singles figure skating program.*

The figure 8 is two perfect circles. Each figure must be skated three times on each foot and the same path, or tracing, must be followed each time.

Young skaters watch a coach skating a figure. School figures count as 30 percent of the singles event score.

The best skaters who compete in the national and international championships are invited by the United States Olympic committee to compete in selection trials. These trials help the committee decide who will have a chance to go to the Olympics. Only the very best skaters go on to Olympic competition. It is the chance of a lifetime for them. They will represent their country and try to be better than the best skaters from many countries in the world.

OLYMPIC COMPETITION

In Olympic competition, as in other championship contests, there are four major events: single men's skating, single women's skating, pairs skating, and ice dancing.

SINGLES SKATING

In the singles events there are three parts: school figures, a short program, and a free-skating program. *School figures* are the first performed. A skater picks three figures from the forty-one figures set up by the ISU as a test of technical skill. The skater then skates each figure (for example, a figure 8) three times on each foot. The skater makes the three figures as alike as possible. He or she must also use the same edge (for example, the outside forward edge) in doing the figure. When the skater has finished, the judges look at the path, or tracing, that is left on the ice. The judges can tell from the tracing if the skater made any mistakes in the figure. In addition, the judges

Dorothy Hamill, at nineteen, won the gold medal at Innsbruck in 1976.

A winning performance.

Dorothy Hamill's famous "Hamill Camel."

Linda Fratianne in a beautiful spin.

watch the skater who is performing the figure to see that the skater is relaxed and looks graceful and effortless while doing the figure. The school figures count as 30 percent of the final score.

The next part of the singles competition is a *short program.* The judges have picked several mandatory moves, such as a flying camel and a sit spin. The skater must work these moves into a two-minute program. The skater and coach together pick the music and the order of moves for the routine. All the moves required by the judges must be included in this program, or points are deducted. This segment of the singles event counts as 20 percent of the total score.

Finally, the skaters perform their *free skating* routines. This is the part of the program that both the skaters and the audience like the best. Men have five minutes and women have four to show the judges their combinations of difficult moves, leaps, and spins, performed to music selected by the skaters. The skaters may combine approved moves or may introduce variations on these moves. Dorothy Hamill, for instance, combined a camel spin with a sit spin in a move that was soon described as a "Hamill camel." The routine is judged on technical excellence as well as gracefulness, power, and fluidity. The skater is expected to use the whole rink for the routine, and the music should be an important, integral part of the program. The free-skating part of the singles program counts for 50 percent of the total score.

Peggy Fleming, United States gold medalist in 1968, demonstrates a layback spin and a cross-foot spin.

Dick Button, United States gold medalist in 1948, shows a winning leap.

FREE-SKATING MOVES

Some of the approved moves that a skater uses in free skating are:

AXEL   A jump in which the skater skates forward, leaps in the air, turns one and a half times, and lands going backward. In a *double axel* the skater turns two and a half times in the air.

CAMEL SPIN   The skater spins with one skate blade flat on the ice (both edges touching the ice) while the other leg and the upper body are held parallel to the ice. In the *flying camel* the skater jumps and immediately starts a camel spin.

CROSS-FOOT SPIN   The skater crosses his or her legs, toes together and heels apart, and spins on the flat of both skates. The cross-foot spin is the fast spin often used at the end of a program.

FLIP JUMP   While skating backward, the skater takes off from the outside edge of one blade, with a push from the toe-point of the other blade, rotates counter-clockwise in the air, and lands on the back outside edge of the other skate blade.

LAYBACK SPIN   The skater spins on one foot while bending backward.

LUTZ   While skating backward, as in the flip jump, the skater jumps from the outside edge of one blade and pushes with the toe-point of the free blade. Instead of rotating counter-clockwise, the skater spins clockwise in the air before landing on the other leg.

SALCHOW   The skater leaps from the outside back edge of the skating foot, turns once in the air, and lands on the outside back edge of the same skating foot. A *double salchow* is two turns in the air.

19

In the 1870s women wore long dresses, even to skate. Pairs skating developed because it was felt that women needed to be protected from becoming entangled in their dresses and possibly falling on the ice.

Tai Babilonia and Randy Gardner, a United States pair couple, in championship form.

SIT SPIN   While standing, the skater begins to spin on one foot and then bends the knee of the skating foot to get to a sitting position, with the free leg extended in front.

SPIRAL   The skater glides either forward or backward on one foot while assuming a graceful pose and holding that pose. The skater looks almost like a statue gliding on the ice.

SPREADEAGLE   The skater turns his or her feet out in either direction and holds that position in a glide, leaning either forward or backward, while making a large arc over the ice. A *spreadeagle jump* is a half-turn jump made while the skater is doing a spreadeagle glide.

THREE-JUMP   While skating forward, the skater jumps off the skating foot, makes a half-turn in the air, and lands going backward on the opposite foot.

PAIRS SKATING

Pairs skating started in England in the late 1800s. At first it was called "hand-in-hand" skating. It began because people felt that women skaters needed to be protected. Women wore long dresses at that time, even to skate. If they became entangled in their dresses and fell, they might be hurt. Also, it was considered a disgrace for a woman to fall down in public. With a partner to help her keep her balance, a woman kept her dignity, too!

Irina Rodnina and Alexei Ulanov of the U.S.S.R. do a death spiral on their way to a gold medal in 1972.

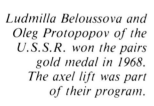

Ludmilla Beloussova and Oleg Protopopov of the U.S.S.R. won the pairs gold medal in 1968. The axel lift was part of their program.

Pairs contests in the Olympic Games are a little like singles contests. The partners, a man and a woman, use the same kinds of moves used by solo skaters. The same kinds of standards also are used to judge pairs. Good techniques and the appearance of relaxation on the ice are important in the skaters' programs. Pairs select their own music and must use the entire rink in their program. The couple may skate together or separately. However, even when they are at opposite ends of the arena, they must always look as if their moves are in harmony.

In Olympic competition, each pair must do a *short compulsory program.* This program includes a number of moves that the judges have selected earlier. This part of the competition counts as 30 percent of the total score.

Pairs also perform a *free-skating routine* that lasts about five minutes. This is probably the most exciting part of the competition. The routines include lifts, in which the man holds his partner over his head. The couple also "shadow skates," which means that they perform the exact same moves while skating separately. The free-skating routine counts as 70 percent of the final score.

Pairs skating includes some very different and exciting moves. In the *death spiral,* the man holds the woman by one of her hands while one skate is on the ice. He spins her around very quickly while staying on the same part of the ice. She leans over backward so that her head is very close to the ice while she is being spun around.

In the *axel lift,* the woman is lifted over the man's head and turned one-and-a-half times in the air. The man is also spinning around while turning her.

23

*Stacey Smith and John Summers,
1979 United States ice dancing
champions, show their vitality.*

Tai Babilonia and Randy Gardner must make identical moves to score high.

In an *arabesque* or *catch-waist camel spin,* the partners perform a camel spin while facing in opposite directions, and hold each other by the waist while spinning.

For the *split lutz lift* the couple skates backward. The woman is lifted over the man's head as she does the splits.

The most difficult part of skating in pairs is making moves exactly together. If both skaters are jumping, each must jump as high as the other and they must land at the same time. Their skating must be as perfect as that of a singles skater, and their moves must be as precisely together as possible.

ICE DANCING

Organized ice dancing started in the late 1800s. Jackson Haines, an American dancer-skater, helped to make it popular. Haines combined ballet with skating and toured Europe giving skating exhibitions. In England, most people turned up their noses at Haines' "fancy skating." In Vienna, Austria, however, it became very popular. Romantic dances such as the waltz were then at the height of their popularity in Vienna. Austrians felt that ice dancing expressed the same kind of flowing, romantic motion.

25

Colleen O'Connor and Jimmy Millns of the United States show their 1976 bronze medal ice-dancing style.

*Danelle Porter and Burt Lancon,
members of the 1979
Junior World ice-dancing team.*

Austrians began to take skating lessons so that they could learn to dance on ice. Ice dancing finally caught on in England in the 1930s. Skaters were very enthusiastic about it, and invented many new dances.

The first ice dancing championship was held in Paris in 1952. The United States held its first championship in 1960.

Ice dancing did not become an Olympic event until 1976. Though many people had tried for years to have it added to the competition, the International Olympic Committee (IOC) had ruled against it. They felt it was not a true sport. Ice dancing will continue to grow in popularity now that the IOC has recognized it as a sport in its own right.

Ice dancing is very different from pairs skating. The man and woman are not permitted to skate separately except to change positions or direction. They do not perform lifts. They may use very few free-skating moves, and only those that look as if they belong in the dance being done.

Ice dancing is ballroom dancing on ice. Instead of learning school figures, ice dancers learn different kinds of dances, such as the waltz or the tango. In competition, couples must perform in three events: compulsory (required) dances, an original set-pattern dance, and free dancing.

Tai Babilonia and Randy Gardner execute a free-dancing move.

In the first event, couples must perform three *compulsory dances* very precisely. The specific group of dances, such as the starlight waltz, the rhumba, and the Argentine tango, are announced earlier. All competing couples must perform these same dances, and they must dance to the same music. The ISU has official dance diagrams that show the exact moves the couple must perform. This event counts as 30 percent of the final score.

The *original set-pattern dance* is chosen and choreographed (composed and arranged) by each couple. However, the judges decide on the kind of music that the couple must dance to. Each couple may arrange the dance as they wish, but must follow the rules of ice dancing very closely. This event counts as 20 percent of the final score.

In the *free-dancing* event each couple performs a series of dances in a four-minute program. They are not permitted to repeat moves, but must show how well they can do many kinds of dances. They choose their own music, but it must have different kinds of beats in it. Each couple's free-dancing program is judged on difficulty, technical performance, variety, and artistic interpretation.

There are more than fifteen standard dances recognized by the ISU. Included are a variety of waltzes, with their "ONE-two-three" beat; the tango, with a "one, two, one-two-three" rhythm; the foxtrot, with a beat of "ONE, two, THREE, four"; and the rumba, with a "ONE, TWO, THREE, four" rhythm.

*Barbara Ann Scott of Canada won the gold in 1948, starting
the shift from European dominance of figure skating.*

SOME FAMOUS OLYMPIC SKATERS

The real story of Olympic skating is in the people who take part in Olympic competition. People from every corner of the world skate in the Olympics and watch the competition. Spectators might want their own countrymen to win, but all are quick to see which athletes deserve their applause. During the Games, people forget national differences and see only excellent athletes trying to be perfect at their sports. At that time each spectator is truly a citizen of the world.

WOMEN **Sonja Heine** of Norway entered international competition in 1924, when she was eleven years old. In the 1924 Winter Olympics Heine shocked the skating world. She wore a short skating costume instead of an ankle-length skirt and in her free-skating program she used spins and jumps that previously had been used only by men. The judges gave her last place.

Four years later, however, she came back to win the first of her ten world championship titles. She was world champion for ten years in a row. In 1928 she won the first of three consecutive gold medals. Sonja Heine dominated women's skating until 1936. Her record of wins has never yet been equaled by another skater.

Because of World War II, no Olympic competitions were held between 1936 and 1948. In 1948 **Barbara Ann Scott** of Canada won the women's singles gold medal, and in the 1952 Olympics the winner was **Jeanette Altweg** of England. In the next Olympic competitions, two skaters from the United States emerged as bright stars of international skating.

31

*Tenley Albright of the United States was a silver medalist in 1952
and a gold medalist in 1956. Currently she is an officer of the 1980
United States Olympic Committee. In private life she is a physician.*

Carol Heiss of the United States won the gold in 1960 with an inspired and harmonious performance.

Tenley Albright began to take intensive skating lessons when she was ten years old. By the time she was sixteen she was on the 1952 United States Olympic team. She took a silver medal that year. In 1953 she won the world championship, the first woman from the United States to take that prize. She lost the title the following year, but came back in 1955 to reclaim her world championship.

In the 1956 Olympics Albright became the first woman skater from the United States to take a gold medal in Olympic competition. After this achievement, she retired from competition to complete her medical studies, setting the stage for another American skater to excel.

Carol Heiss entered international competition in 1953. She had competed with Tenley Albright many times, but was always a runner-up. When Albright retired, Heiss became the star of the American team. In 1956 she won both a silver medal in the Olympics and the world championship. She remained world champion for four straight years.

She was ready for the 1960 Olympics. With her excellent sense of music and her mature, inspiring performance, she beat Sjoukje Dijkstra of the Netherlands to take the gold medal. Some time later she retired from competition and married Hayes Jenkins, the men's national figure-skating champion from the United States. The prince and princess of skating ended their fairy-tale careers.

Peggy Fleming, United States gold medalist in 1968, won through her technical and ballet movements, which brought her very high scores.

Left to right: Karen Magnussen, Canada—silver; Trixi Schuba, Austria—gold; Janet Lynn, United States—bronze. 1972 Olympic results.

In 1961 a terrible accident took place. The United States Olympic figure-skating team was flying to Czechoslovakia to compete in the world championships. The plane crashed in Belgium, killing everyone on board. Because the best skaters in the United States had died, many people believed it would take a long time to build up another team that was as good. But these people were wrong.

Sjoukje Dijkstra, the Dutch skater who had lost to Carol Heiss in 1960, took the gold medal in the 1964 Olympics. Placing sixth in that contest was an American girl named **Peggy Fleming.** Fleming was destined to be the next United States superstar skater.

By the time Peggy Fleming began to skate in international competitions, she was no longer the little girl who fell down in every sport she tried. Her pretty "ballerina" skating won her the world championships in 1966 and 1967. She topped this achievement by winning the gold medal in the 1968 Olympics. Fleming was truly an "international" champion. She had as many fans in Europe as she did in the United States.

In the next Olympics, in 1972, Austrian **Trixi Schuba** won the gold medal. Her perfection in school figures gave her the edge she needed to win. **Karen Magnusson,** the excellent Canadian skater, took the silver medal, and **Janet Lynn** of the United States took the bronze. Lynn had been favored to win the gold, but a fall during her free-skating routine robbed her of the points she needed to win.

Dick Button invented several jumps that are now part of Olympic routines.

A new United States star shone in the 1976 Winter Olympics. **Dorothy Hamill's** bright smile and sparkling personality filled the arena. Her skating was daring and athletic. Hamill was the gold medalist that year. In addition, she won the world championship contest about a month later.

Dorothy Hamill became a professional skater after winning these honors, leaving the door open for her successor. Who will it be?

MEN Until 1948, men's international skating competitions were dominated by European skaters. Some of the greatest included **Ulrich Salchow** of Sweden. He was the world champion ten times and inventor of the salchow jump. **Gillis Grafstrom,** also from Sweden, won three Olympic gold medals, and **Karl Schafer** of Austria was the Olympic gold medalist in both 1932 and 1936.

By the time World War II had ended and the Olympic Games were held again, a United States skater was ready to revolutionize men's skating.

Dick Button was sixteen in 1946 when he won the United States national championship. He was the youngest man ever to win this title. Two years later, in 1948, he won his first world championship and his first Olympic gold medal. Button was an unusually athletic skater. He combined double and triple spins with difficult leaps and jumps. One of his career highlights was his gold-medal performance in the 1952 Olympics. In that competition he performed a triple jump (three revolutions in the air). At one time Button held five titles at once, a record that has never been repeated. He turned professional after the 1952 Olympics. Succeeding him were two brothers also destined for skating history.

37

Hayes Allen Jenkins, United States gold medalist in 1956, married Carol Heiss.

David Jenkins, United States gold medalist in 1960, is the brother of Hayes Allen Jenkins.

Kenneth Shelley of the United States placed fourth in the 1972 Olympics.

Hayes Allen Jenkins and **David Jenkins** were the top United States figure skaters for a period of eight years. Hayes was the United States national champion from 1953 through 1956. He capped this brilliant career by taking the gold medal in the 1956 Olympics. His brother David succeeded him in the United States national championship, winning it from 1957 through 1960. David won the Olympic bronze the same year that Hayes won his gold. In the next Olympiad David won his own gold medal. David's excellent free-skating performance in the 1960 competition made many people think he might be the best skater in history.

After David Jenkins's win in 1960, men's Olympic skating was again swept by European performers. In 1964 **Manfred Schnelldorfer** of West Germany took the gold; in 1968 it was **Wolfgang Schwartz** of Austria. In the 1972 Olympics **Ondrej Nepela** of Czechoslovakia was brilliant in both his compulsory figures and his free skating, and took home a well-deserved gold medal. In 1976 **John Curry** of Great Britain performed a flawless free-skating routine that made him the top Olympic winner. The fact that no one country has established a pattern of producing Olympic figure-skating champions makes the outcome of the next Olympic Games even more suspenseful.

PAIRS In past Olympics certain countries have produced either strong pairs skaters or strong individual skaters. Pairs skaters from Germany, France, Canada, Hungary, and the U.S.S.R. have won many championships.

*Ludmilla Beloussova and Oleg
Protopopov of the U.S.S.R. won gold medals
for pairs skating in 1964 and 1968.*

Heinrich Burger and **Anna Hubler,** from Germany, had the honor of winning the first Olympic gold medal in 1908.

A husband-and-wife team, **Andree** and **Pierre Brunet** of France, earned two gold medals and a bronze medal during their skating days. Pierre later became a skating coach. One of his best pupils was Carol Heiss of the United States, the gold medalist in 1960.

A truly outstanding couple from the U.S.S.R., **Oleg Protopopov** and his wife **Ludmilla Belousova,** set the pace at both the 1964 and 1968 Olympics. They were unbeatable, and won gold medals in both years. The Protopopovs did not include daring, athletic "tricks" in their routines. They were absolutely perfect in every move they made, and won many championships because of this.

Another couple from the U.S.S.R., **Irina Rodnina** and **Alexei Ulanov,** won the gold medal in 1972. They did not work together as well as everyone expected them to, however. The reason for this became clear when Alexei married another skater from the U.S.S.R., **Ludmilla Smirnova,** and Irina became the wife of **Aleksandr Zaitsev,** also a skater. At the 1972 Olympics the pairs skaters used more spectacular moves than ever before. They were moving away from the style of the Protopopovs into a more athletic style.

In 1976, Irina Rodnina came back to the Olympics with a new partner, her husband Aleksandr Zaitsev, to take another gold medal. This time the partners showed an amazing degree of harmony. Their solo jumps and spins were timed perfectly, and their lifts were graceful and looked effortless.

41

Ludmilla Pakhomova and Alexandr Gorshkov of the U.S.S.R. won the first gold medal ever given for ice dancing.

Colleen O'Connor and Jimmy Millns of the United States.

JoJo Starbuck and Kenneth Shelley of the United States placed fourth in the 1972 Olympics pairs competition.

In the Olympics of 1980 it will be interesting to see if the skaters from the U.S.S.R. continue to dominate the pairs skating event. Both pairs skating and ice dancing are very popular in the U.S.S.R. Which couple will dazzle Olympic audiences at Lake Placid?

ICE DANCING Since ice dancing was a new event in the 1976 Olympics, only three couples have had the chance to become medalists. The U.S.S.R. did very well in this first contest, taking first, second, and fourth place. **Ludmilla Pakhomova** and **Aleksandr Gorshkov** were the first gold-medal winners with their graceful, harmonious style. The couple who danced their way to third place for a bronze medal were **Colleen O'Connor** and **Jimmy Millns,** the national ice-dancing champions from the United States. Ice dancing will be an exciting event to look forward to in the next Olympics.

43

Tai Babilonia and Randy Gardner, United States national pairs champions in 1979.

Left to right: David Santee, Charlie Tickner, and Scott Cramer, members of the United States figure skating team, each have hopes for a medal in the 1980 Winter Olympics.

Linda Fratianne of the United States won her third national title in 1979.

Scott Cramer is a member of the 1980 United States Olympic figure skating team.

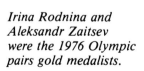

Irina Rodnina and Aleksandr Zaitsev were the 1976 Olympic pairs gold medalists.

*Left to right: Vladimir Kovalev, U.S.S.R.,
John Curry, Great Britain, and Toller
Cranston, Canada, 1976 Olympic medal winners.*

*Charlie Tickner of the United States
is a member of the 1980 Olympic team.*

OLYMPIC GOLD MEDALISTS

Figure Skating — Men

Year	Name	Country
1924	Gillis Grafstrom	Sweden
1928	Gillis Grafstrom	Sweden
1932	Karl Schafer	Austria
1936	Karl Schafer	Austria
1948	Richard Button	United States
1952	Richard Button	United States
1956	Hayes Alan Jenkins	United States
1960	David Jenkins	United States
1964	Manfred Schnelldorfer	Germany
1968	Wolfgang Schwarz	Austria
1972	Ondrej Nepela	Czechoslovakia
1976	John Curry	Great Britain

Figure Skating — Women

Year	Name	Country
1924	Herma Planck-Szabo	Austria
1928	Sonja Henie	Norway
1932	Sonja Henie	Norway
1936	Sonja Henie	Norway
1948	Barbara Scott	Canada
1952	Jeanette Altwegg	Great Britain
1956	Tenley Albright	United States
1960	Carol Heiss	United States
1964	Sjoukje Dijkstra	Netherlands
1968	Peggy Gale Fleming	United States
1972	Beatrix Schuba	Austria
1976	Dorothy Hamill	United States

OLYMPIC GOLD MEDALISTS

Figure Skating — Pairs

Year	Name	Country
1924	Helene Engelmann and Alfred Berger	Austria
1928	Andree Joly and Pierre Brunet	France
1932	Andree and Pierre Brunet	France
1936	Maxie Herber and Ernst Baier	Germany
1948	Micheline Lannoy and Pierre Baugniet	Belgium
1952	Ria and Paul Falk	Germany
1956	Elisabeth Schwarz and Kurt Oppelt	Austria
1960	Barbara Wagner and Robert Paul	Canada
1964	Ludmilla Beloussova and Oleg Protopopov	U.S.S.R.
1968	Ludmilla Beloussova and Oleg Protopopov	U.S.S.R.
1972	Irina Rodnina and Alexei Ulanov	U.S.S.R.
1976	Irina Rodnina and Alexandr Zaitsev	U.S.S.R.

Ice Dancing — Pairs

Year	Name	Country
1976	Ludmilla Pakhomova, Alexander Gorshkov	U.S.S.R.

48